I am amazed

jodi hills

Waldman House Press
Minneapolis

This book is dedicated to my mother, Ivy, who amazes me every day by being my best friend. I'm lucky, because I see her in every page. If you're lucky, you'll see your family and friends here too, and even better, they'll see you.

jodi hills

Library of Congress Cataloging-in-Publication Data

Hills, Jodi, 1968-
I am amazed: take a look around and you will be too / Jodi Hills.
p. cm.
ISBN 0-931674-51-4 (alk.paper)
1. Conduct of life--Miscellanea. I. Title.
BJ1595 .H6215 2002
158.2--dc21   2002016844

Waldman House Press is an imprint of TRISTAN Publishing, Inc.

Waldman House Press
2300 Louisiana Avenue North, Suite B
Golden Valley, MN 55427

It wasn't that Fred Astaire did things that no one else could or can... but it was the ease in each step, the seemingly effortless grace that carried him... that's what I admire.

As one who stumbles
over my own heart and
mind every day,

I am amazed and filled with admiration for those Astaire-like qualities that dance all around me.

I admire those
who wake each
morning and find
a reason to smile,

and then give you
theirs for no reason
at all.

I am amazed by
those who show up,
who reach out,
and who look
within.

I admire those who say hello and goodbye with the same sincerity and sensitivity.

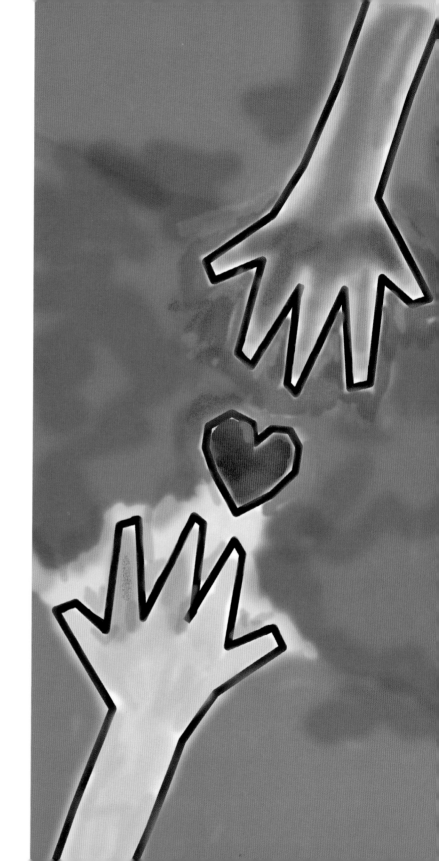

I admire those
who are afraid to
take the journey,
but still open
the door.

I admire those
on the other side
who let you in
and offer you
to stay.

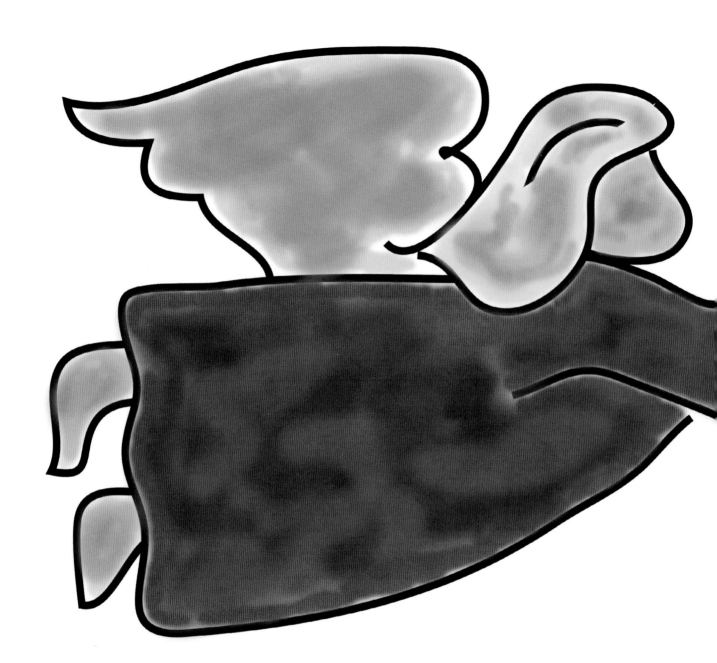

I admire those
who touch
without harm.

I admire the fool
who attempts what
the intelligent are
afraid to try.

I admire the
vulnerable hero,

those unwilling
to be victims,

and the losers
who play again
and again, just
for fun.

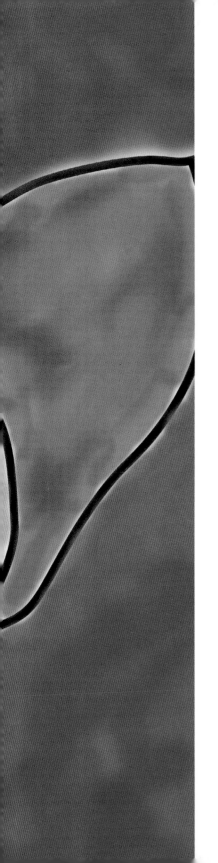

I admire those
who plant,
who nurture,
who create,
and grow.

I admire the patient who take risks, and the risk-takers with patience.

I am amazed by
those who walk
the daily high-rope
without looking down.

I admire those
who trust,

and even more,
those who give
us reason to.

I admire those who
give direction without
"should have"s and
"supposed to"s.

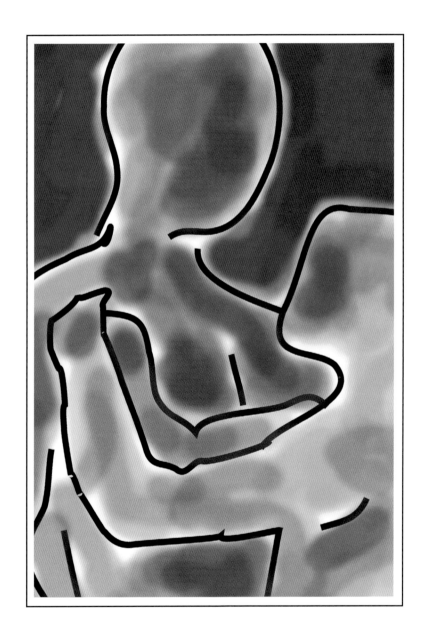

I admire the builders...
and I am amazed
by those who have
the strength to rebuild.

I admire the
teachers who
listen, and the
listeners who then
teach.

I am amazed by
the resilience of the
faithful,
        those who believe
with no proof,
and those who sing
with no audience.

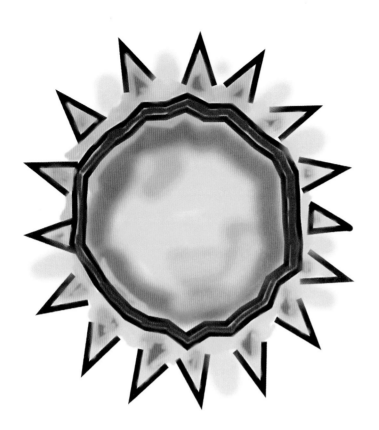

I admire the strength
of the honest,
    and the courage
of those willing
to share their story.

I admire those
who forgive,

and I am amazed
by those who
have forgiven me.

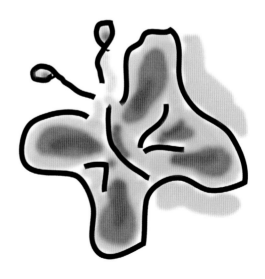

I am amazed
at the wisdom
of the young and
the playfulness of
the aged, and I
admire those who
dare the untimely
roles of each.

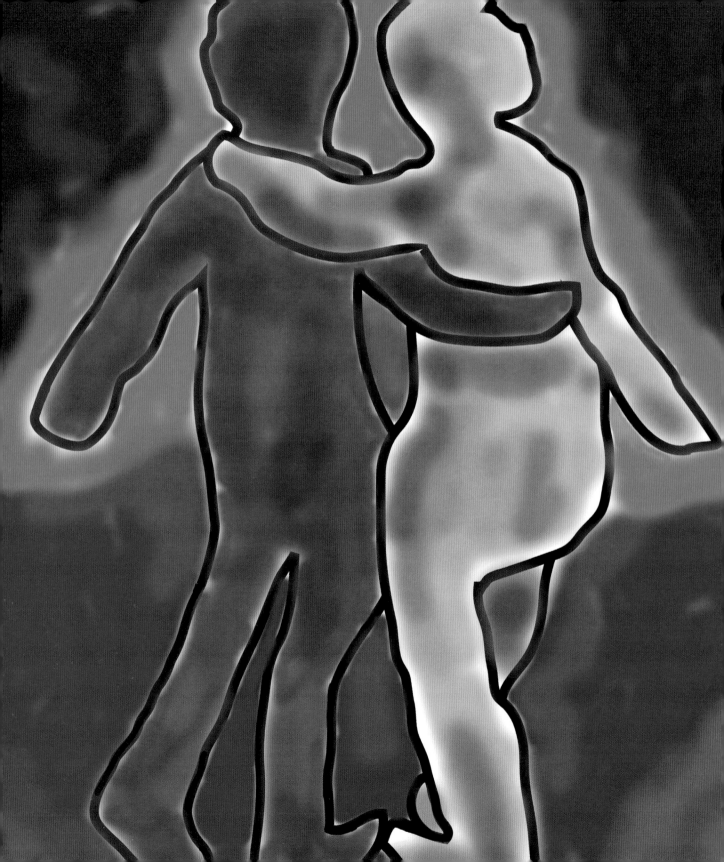

I admire the loyal,
the friend who sees
the person, and not
the situation or the
opportunity.

I admire the helpful, and bravery of those unafraid to ask for their assistance,

each humbly knowing
that the roles could be
reversed at any given
moment.

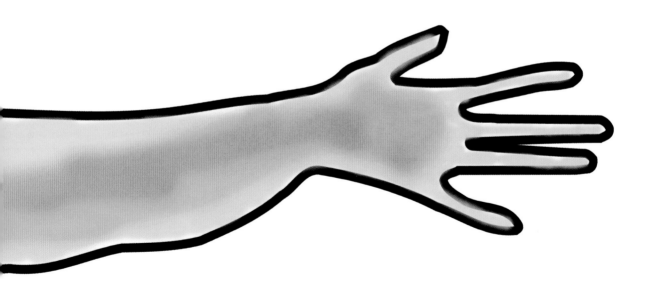

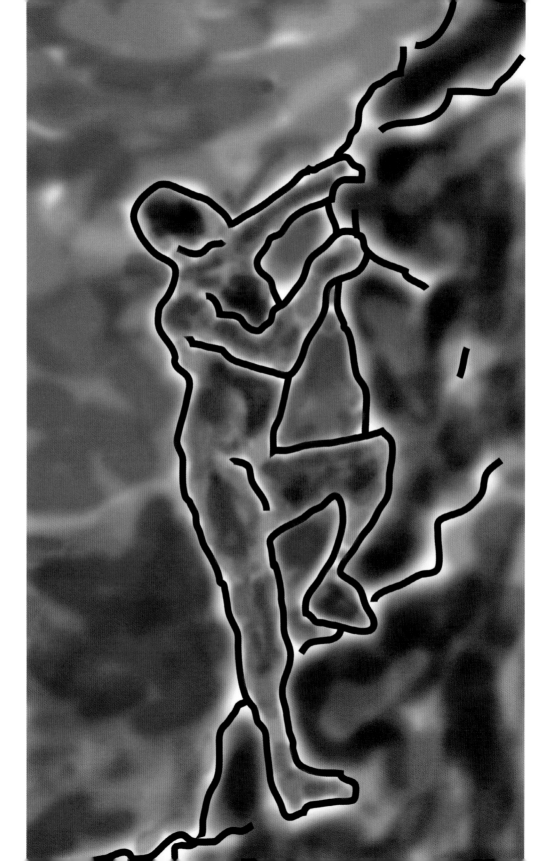

I admire those who
remember and remind,
and still have the
drive to move ahead.

I admire the lost
who keep looking,
and I'm amazed
by those who keep
looking for the
lost.

I am amazed by those who go to sleep with nothing and carry the sweetest dreams.

Mostly I admire you,

you who give love
so effortlessly,
with such ease, and
such grace... as if
the steps of the
heart just flowed
from your every
muscle,

and I am amazed that you let
me fumble along beside you.

It's you who
amaze me...

you lovers
and losers,

you teachers
and listeners,

you faithful and
hopeful spirits of
playfulness, wisdom
and strength...

you who show up
every day and
dance.